Homestyle Icelandic Cooking
for
American Kitchens

Heidi Herman and Íeda Jónasdóttir Herman

Homestyle Icelandic Cooking for American Kitchens

DepositPhotos: vvoennyy
Cover by Kelly A. Martin

Copyright © 2016 by Heidi Herman
V2.0 r1.0

All rights reserved. No part of this book may be reproduced, or transmitted in any form or by any means, electronic or mechanical, to include photocopying, recording, or by any informational storage or retrieval system, without the written permission of the Author, except where permitted by law.

First Edition

Paperback ISBN: 978-1-947233-05-8
Hardcover ISBN: 978-1-947233-90-4

Hekla Publishing and the Hekla logo are trademarks belonging to Hekla Publishing LLC

DEDICATION

This is dedicated to all those researching their roots, reconnecting with their heritage or connecting for the first time with Icelandic culture and food. May these recipes find their way into your heart through your stomach – by way of the dinner table, cookie jar, potluck dinner, bake sales and special celebrations.

Cultures are born and die, but the cheese is immortal. – Icelandic Proverb

CONTENTS

Introduction		1
History of Icelandic Food		5
Pronunciation Guide		9
Remoulade	- Remoulade (Brown Sauce)	10
Mýsuostur	- Brown Whey Cheese	12
Brúnar Kartöflur	- Brown Potatoes	14
Rófa	- Rutabaga	16
Kjötsúpa	- Meat Soup	18
Plokkfiskur	- Fish Stew	20
Fiskur Með Ostur	- Cheesy Fish	22
Fiska Bollur	- Fish Balls	24
Bakaður Fiskur	- Baked Fish	26
Flatkökur	- Flatbread	28
Rúgbrauð Svart	- Black (Rye) Bread	30
Rúgbrauð Brúnt	- Brown (Rye) Bread	32
Litlabollur	- Doughnut Balls	34
Kleinur	- Kleinur (Doughnut)	36

Piparkökur	- Pepper Cookie	38
Parisarkökur	- Meringue Cookie	40
Vanilluhringir	- Vanilla Ring Cookie	42
Mömmukökur	- Mama's Cookie	44
Smjörkrem	- Butter Icing	46
Bolludagur Bollur	- Buns (Cream Puff)	48
Rjómaterta	- Whipped Cream Cake	50
Vínarterta	- Vienna Cake	52
Fyltur Hveitibrauðskrans	- Coffee Wreath	56
Vínarbrauð I	- Vienna Bread (pastry) #1	58
Vínarbrauð II	- Vienna Bread (pastry) #2	60
Vínarbrauð III	- Vienna Bread (pastry) #3	62
Púðingur Fylta	- Custard Filling	64
Pönnukökur	- Pancakes	66

INTRODUCTION

As I was growing up, my Mother's Icelandic heritage was not something I thought much about, although the story was something I was very familiar with. She was born in Reykjavik, Iceland in 1925. My father served in the Navy during WWII and was stationed in Iceland. They met at a USO dance and were married in Iceland in 1945 and, after the war, they settled in the US. Her nationality was somewhat unusual and she spoke with a unique and beautifully distinctive accent. I loved to hear her speak Icelandic, although I didn't understand what she said. As a young girl, I was more interested in other activities and regrettably didn't put the time in to learn Icelandic.

One of the activities I was more interested in was cooking. In elementary school, somewhere around fifth grade, I acquired my first cookbook. As I recall, it was a cookie cookbook and I enjoyed carefully following the directions for each one. I quickly developed a love of baking, particularly desserts, that has lasted a lifetime.

My first venture into something a bit more complicated ended in a messy disaster. Although, looking back, it should not have been a complicated undertaking. I remember calling my Mom at work to ask her how to make mashed potatoes. She walked me through the steps of peeling, and listed off the necessary ingredients of butter, milk and the salt.

My young ears must have missed the part about boiling the potatoes. When I put the hand mixer into the pan and flipped it on high speed, a cascade of milk, lumps of butter, and chunks of potato flew into the air, splattering the cabinet-fronts and walls and stuck in little bits to the 70s-era popcorn ceiling. That ceiling was never the same. I have had a strict policy ever since to follow written recipes. I will, however, make notes and alterations as I add recipes to my collection. Over time, I acquired hundreds of recipes for appetizers, entrees, cookies, and all sorts of desserts.

As an adult, I came to appreciate the unique history and rich heritage I had in my Icelandic ancestry. I made my first trip to Iceland when I was in my early 20's. It was a family trip with my parents and several of my sisters. We met and visited with Icelandic relatives, and toured the country by driving the Ring Road. I purchased a Terta Cookie that was nearly 8" in diameter and snacked on it for days. I remember the layers of crisp cookie, jam filling, and pink icing coating on top. I thought it was delicious fantastic and like nothing I had tasted before. During the trip, I tasted sea bass for the first time, as well as white asparagus, mutton and a few other unidentified selections. I found the cuisine was very different than what I used to and definitely foreign.

In subsequent trips, I developed an appreciation for the Icelandic flavors and the understated desserts. The pastries, cakes and desserts are made with more dairy than sugar, resulting in a richer, but less sweet taste. Ingredients such as milk, butter, and eggs were more readily available than sugar or other sweeteners and those portions are reflected in the recipes. It is difficult to find many of the traditional recipes in English, and those that have been translated are often presented with measurements in metric.

I undertook this project to be able to create some of my favorite Icelandic treats in my American kitchen. My goal was to have the recipes and instructions to make kleinur or a terta as easily as I would muffins or an apple pie. I knew I couldn't do it by myself, so I enlisted my Mom's help. She has always loved to share her Icelandic heritage and I knew she truly missed having kleinur stocked in the freezer.

In the making of this cookbook, Mom and I had a great partnership. She assisted in translating the recipes from Icelandic to English and I converted measurements from metric to American standard. Some ingredients needed to be changed and processes clarified and some measurements even defined. One recipe was two lines long and simply translated to "mix all ingredients and cook in hot oven".

I tested each of the recipes and she sampled to determine if they were as she remembered. It became a lengthy process and some recipes required more alterations than others. As I researched, I came across a few dishes that were unknown to her. I found it difficult to properly assess the results Mom and I were sampling. I would constantly say, "OK, it tastes good, but does it taste *right*?" whereupon she would answer, "I'm not sure, I don't remember having this back then." As a result, during our 2016 annual trip to Iceland, I found myself stopping at every bakarí we came across, constantly sampling baked goods, cakes and cookies.

After much sampling and taste testing, Mom and I are now confident that all the recipes in this collection will produce main dishes, breads and desserts that are accurate and have the proper Icelandic flavors. The collection does not cover all traditional Icelandic dishes, but we included many of our personal favorites.

Please enjoy!

A Brief History and Overview of Icelandic Food

The standard fare in Iceland is simple nourishing foods. Many of the best recipes are very simple dishes, and that's part of what makes them so appealing. Throughout the settlement history and into early this century, the focus of everyone's time was on work. Most of the most common dishes take few ingredients and limited preparation time. They could be eaten quickly or even while continuing to work. Breads are hearty and filling, snacks can be carried in a pocket or knapsack and many baked goods have a very long storage life.

Meals were rarely eaten together as a family. It was common for a pot of soup to continually be simmering on the back of the stove. Family members and hired hands would help themselves to a bowl when they could take a break from the work. The soup, along with a slab of bread would serve as a quick meal. On the way out the door, it was typical to grab two or three kleinur to stick in a pocket for later. "Harðfiskur" or dried fish was often carried with bread to eat while working. Dried fish is still a common snack today, available at most grocery and convenience stores.

The mainstay of the Icelandic diet has always been fish, and historically, there were limited options for side dishes. Potatoes, rutabaga, carrots, beets and cabbage are common. Typically, these would be boiled or prepared in a similar simple manner with few ingredients. There is very little use of gravies or sauces in any of the dishes.

Because dairy and eggs were more plentiful, the traditional desserts and confections are more rich than sweet. Sugar was in limited supply and the recipes reflect a more generous use of butter, milk, sour cream, and buttermilk. This makes for very rich and filling desserts that are not overly-sweet.

There is some borrowing of recipes within Scandinavia – Icelanders have close family ties to Norway and Denmark and some of the recipes are reminiscent of those countries. In this century, more ingredients have become available and there has been more influence from outside sources, so some of the more modern recipes use spices or ingredients not commonly found in the older recipes.

Traditional Icelandic food

In the early settlement days life was hard and food was often in short supply. Because of this, every part of the animal or fish was used in some way. In this time, there were limited means for preservation of meat and other perishables. Many of Iceland's current processes have roots in the Viking era traditions of preservation.

A traditional curing method used for a variety of meats and fish is refered to as "þorramatur". During January and February, many of these foods are served in a buffet during Þorrablót festivals, the mid-winter feast celebrating the old culture.

Proteins & Meats

Fish has always been the most common Icelandic meal, due to the plentiful fishing. Haddock, halibut, herring, and shrimp are common as well as shark and seal. Meats such as lamb, mutton and beef were typically reserved for special occasions. There was no small game indigenous to the island to hunt for meat, only sea birds.

Raising sheep has been a core part of the Icelandic lifestyle, however they were primarily raised for wool rather than as a food source. Similarly, nearly every farm had a bull, heifers and several milk cows, but they were rarely slaughtered for food.

Birds are plentiful throughout Iceland and, as such, are a core part of the diet, particularly sea birds. Historically, chickens were kept for their eggs and were rarely eaten. Other fowl such as duck or turkey were not common until as late as this century. Today, duck and turkey as well as beef, pork, lamb and mutton are all common and readily available.

Dairy

The calcium-rich diet relies heavily on dairy and is a large part of Icelandic cooking. Recipes liberally use butter, milk, cream and buttermilk. Skyr is an Icelandic product that has been prevalent for over 1,000 years, the dates back to the Viking settlers. Skyr is similar to Greek yogurt but has a milder flavor and is technically a soft form of cheese. It was traditionally served cold with a topping of milk and sugar. It can be eaten plain as yogurt, as a topping for oatmeal, or mixed with fruit as a dessert. The thick consistency also makes it good for smoothies.

The whey left over from skyr-making was often used to make Mysuostur, a very sweet, soft brown cheese. Mysuostur was typically used as a topping on bread. It is not common today and can be found only in specialty stores.

Fruits & Vegetables

Since the time of the settlement, few vegetables have been grown in Iceland. Gardens are typically limited to potatoes, rutabaga, turnips, carrots, cabbage, and rhubarb. Until recent times, salads were very uncommon and today, produce such as lettuce, tomatoes and peppers are grown in a hothouse or imported.

All fruit was historically imported, with plums and prunes the most popular items. Today, some varieties are grown locally in hothouses. There are, however, many berries, such as blueberries and crowberries, that grow wild in Iceland. Every fall, they are gathered to make jellies and jams. Berry-picking has been a tradition for generations and is still a common practice today.

ICELANDIC PRONUNCIATION GUIDE

The Icelandic language can be difficult to master and many of the unfamiliar characters make it impossible to sound out words properly. The guide below will help with the proper pronunciation of the unique letters. Stress is always on the first syllable of the word (with the notable exception of halló).

Áá	say like in	ouch - how
Ðð	say like in	this - the
Éé	say like in	yet - yell
Íí	say like in	eek - eel
Óó	say like in	over - no
Úú	say like in	loot - moot
Þþ	say like in	thing - thorn
Æœ	say like in	I - Ice
Öö	say like in	hurry – hurt

The letters "C", "Q", "W", and "Z" are not present in the Icelandic alphabet.

The spelling "Iceland" is the English interpretation of the actual name "Ísland".

Remoulade

This a popular condiment for sandwiches and hot dogs but is a tasty sauce over potatoes as well

Ingredients

3/4 cup grapeseed or canola oil

1 egg yolk

1 teaspoon Dijon mustard

1 tablespoon white wine vinegar

2 teaspoons chopped pickle

2 teaspoons horseradish

1 tablespoon chopped parsley

Instructions

1. In a medium bowl, blend the egg yolk and mustard using a wire whisk.

2. *Very slowly* add the oil, blending until smooth and thick.

3. Add the white wine vinegar, chopped pickle, horseradish, and parsley. Blend completely.

4. Store in a tightly sealed container in refrigerator.

Alternatives & Substitutions

A traditional Icelandic mix would typically call for gherkin, capers, and chervil. You can substitute the same measure: 2 teaspoons gherkin in place of the pickle, 2 teaspoons capers for the horseradish or 1 tablespoon chervil in place of the parsley.

Yield approximately 1 cup

Mysuostur

A traditional sweet soft brown cheese. The flavor is a bit like caramel with a texture similar to peanut butter. This sweet spread is a perfect topping for Icelandic black bread.

Ingredients & Instruction I (Traditional)

1 1/2 gallons of liquid whey*

1/4 cup brown sugar

2 tablespoons cream

1/2 teaspoon salt

2 tablespoons butter

Pour whey into large pan or stockpot, add salt and cover. Gradually bring to a full boil and remove cover. Boil uncovered until mixture has reduced by two-thirds, about 5-6 hours. Remove from heat.

Add the butter and cream and mix well. Add sugar and stir until blended. Return to heat and bring to a full boil, stirring constantly. Lower heat to medium and boil, stirring occasionally, for 45-60 minutes or until cheese begins to thicken and turn a light golden brown. Remove from heat, stir vigorously and let cool. When cooled, it should be the consistency of creamy peanut butter.

Refrigerate in jars or a bowl. Yield approximately 2 cups.

Ingredients & Instruction II (Powdered Whey)

- 1 cup water
- 1 1/2 cups powdered milk
- 1/2 tablespoon nutmeg
- 1 1/2 tablespoon lemon juice
- 3/4 cup canola oil
- 2 cups unflavored powdered whey
- 1 1/4 cups brown sugar
- 1 teaspoon baking soda

In large saucepan for double boiler, blend the water, canola oil, and powdered milk until smooth, using wire whisk or electric mixer. Add powdered whey and nutmeg then mix well. Gradually add the brown sugar, lemon juice and baking soda, mixing until the texture is smooth. Set saucepan in double boiler over low heat for 45-60 minutes, stirring occasionally. Cook until mixture resembles smooth peanut butter. Remove from heat, beat well and cool. Store in jar or covered bowl in refrigerator.

Ingredients & Instructions III (Quick Copycat)

- 8 ounce package cream cheese, at room temperature
- 1 tablespoons butter
- 2 tablespoons brown sugar

Lightly caramelize the brown sugar in butter, taking care not to burn it. Cool slightly. In a small bowl, place cream cheese and add the sugar mixture. Beat until creamy.

Alternatives & Substitutions

Powdered (unflavored) whey can be bought at most health food stores. Liquid whey is more uncommon; the best option may be a small local cheese producer.

Brúnar Kartöflur

This simple side dish of potatoes is a traditional favorite – so easy and delicious

Ingredients

- 4-5 medium white potatoes
- 1/2 teaspoon salt
- 1/4 cup butter
- 2 tablespoons sugar

Potatoes grown in Iceland are typically smaller than American-grown potatoes. The size and shape are closer to new red potatoes.

Instructions

1. Peel potatoes and cut into 3" pieces.

2. Fill a medium saucepan with water and add salt. Bring water to a boil.

3. Add potatoes and boil approximately 15-18 minutes, until cooked but not soft.

4. Drain water from potatoes using a colander. Cool potatoes slightly by running cold water over and allow to drain through the colander. Set aside.

5. In a medium-size frying pan, melt butter using high heat. When butter just starts to turn light brown, lower heat to medium and add sugar. Stirring constantly, cook for 1-2 minutes to caramelize. Mixture will turn a golden brown.

6. Add potatoes and allow to cook for 1-2 minutes, turn and coat all sides. Continue cooking until all sides are golden.

7. Garnish with fresh parsley before serving.

Alternatives & Substitutions

Yield 3-4 servings

Rófa

A common vegetable with any meal, rutabaga is served hot or cold, with traditional Þorri foods

Ingredients

2 pounds rutabagas (roughly one large rutabaga)

Salted water

1 cup milk

3 tablespoons butter

1/4 teaspoon salt

1/4 teaspoon pepper

1/4 teaspoon sugar

Instructions

1. Wash and peel rutabagas, chopping into 3"-4" pieces.
2. Rinse in cold water.
3. In a medium saucepan, bring 2-3 cups of salted water to a boil.
4. Add the chopped rutabagas and cook until soft
5. Remove from heat, drain and mash completely. Set aside.
6. In a medium saucepan, melt the butter.
7. Add the rutabaga and stir in half the milk. Over low heat, cook and continue to add as much milk as needed to achieve the consistency of smooth mashed potatoes.
8. Add salt, pepper and sugar.
9. Serve warm or cold

Alternatives & Substitutions

Yield 2-3 servings

Kjötsúpa

This traditional meat soup would often simmer all day and be ladled out anytime during the day

Ingredients

2 pounds lamb shoulder (preferably with some bone) or substitute 3 pounds of beef, cubed

6 cups water or beef bullion

2 teaspoons salt

1/2 teaspoon pepper

1 – 2 tablespoons each of parsley, thyme, bay, and celery, flavored to taste

1 chopped leek

1 large rutabaga, peeled and chopped

1 1/2 cups chopped carrots

2 –3 large potatoes, peeled and chopped

1 cup chopped green cabbage

Instructions

1. Place chopped meat in a large stockpot with 6 cups cold water. Slowly bring to a boil.

2. Add salt, pepper, leek, and seasonings. Simmer, partly covered, for about 45 minutes.

3. Chop the rutabaga, carrots and potatoes and add to the soup. Simmer for about 15 minutes.

4. Add the cabbage and simmer for 5 to 10 minutes, or until all the vegetables are tender.

5. If using bone, lift from the soup, and separate out the bones, sinew and excess fat. Chop up the meat and add them back into the soup. If needed, add a cup or two of more water, and seasoning to taste.

6. Let soup sit overnight for flavors to develop. Garnish with fresh parsley or chives.

Alternatives & Substitutions

The rutabaga can be replaced with turnips and well as the leeks for onion. Traditional Icelandic spices include arctic thyme, birch leaves, bog bilberry, bilberry and juniper. **Add 1/2 cup of** rolled oats, barley, or brown rice to create a thicker soup. This recipe lends itself well to crockpot.

Yield 4-6 servings

Plokkfiskur

A very traditional creamy fish and potato "stew", this casserole-style dish is fast and easy to prepare

Ingredients

1 1/4 pounds cod, halibut, haddock or other type of fish fillets

4-5 potatoes, peeled and chopped

1 white onion, diced

1 1/2 cup milk

4 tablespoons butter

3 tablespoons flour

Salt and pepper to taste

Chives for garnish

Instructions

1. Peel potatoes, chop into quarters and boil until soft.

2. Break up the fish fillets into flakes, set aside.

3. In a large, deep frying pan or skillet, melt butter then add onion. Over medium heat, sauté onion until soft. Do not brown. Add the flour, stir until mixed and let cook for 1-2 minutes.

4. In a small saucepan, heat milk almost to a boiling point. Remove from heat and gradually add milk to onions, stirring continuously.

5. Simmer for 3-4 minutes, stirring often.

6. Add flaked fish and stir briskly to break up the fish flakes completely. Season liberally with salt and pepper.

7. Cook over low heat for 3-4 minutes.

8. Remove potatoes from heat, drain and add to the fish. Stir gently.

9. Sprinkle with chives before serving.

10. Serve hot with dark rye bread and butter.

Alternatives & Substitutions

Yield 3-4 servings

Fiskur Með Ostur

Baked fish is a standard fare, but this dish adds a cheesy twist and is so easy to make

Ingredients

6 fillet of cod or other type of fish

1 lemon

Salt and pepper to taste

1 cup grated Swiss cheese

1 tablespoon mustard

1 cup cream

1/2 cup bread crumbs

Instructions

1. Preheat oven to 375°

2. Prepare a large baking dish by greasing bottom and sides with butter or use nonstick cooking spray.

3. Place the fillets flat in a single layer in the prepared dish. Sprinkle with salt, pepper and freshly squeezed lemon juice.

4. Cover with grated cheese.

5. In a small bowl, combine the mustard with the cream and mix well. Pour over fish cheese layer.

6. Sprinkle with bread crumbs.

7. Bake for 35 minutes.

Alternatives & Substitutions

In place of the Swiss, make with any fondue-type cheese.

Serve with rice, noodles or mashed potatoes.

Yield 6 servings

Fiska Bollar

A classic Icelandic dish, fish is minced and mixed with seasonings and lightly fried.

Ingredients

1 1/2 pound haddocks or other type of fish fillets

1 medium onion, finely chopped

2-3 teaspoons salt

1/6 teaspoon pepper

2 1/2 tablespoons flour

1 tablespoon cornstarch

1 egg

1 cup milk

Oil for frying

Instructions

1. Mince fish and onions and mix together in a medium bowl.
2. Blend in flour, cornstarch, eggs, salt, and pepper.
3. Add milk gradually and stir well.
4. Cover and refrigerate for 30 minutes to thicken.
5. When set, scoop by tablespoonful and form into rounded balls.
6. On stovetop, fry in 2-3" of hot oil, turning until lightly browned on all sides.

Curry Cream Sauce

- 3 tablespoons butter
- ¼ cup flour
- 1 ½ cups milk
- salt and pepper to taste
- ¼ teaspoon curry

In a small skillet over medium heat, melt butter with salt, pepper, and curry. Sprinkle in flour and whisk until smooth. Slowly add milk, continuing to whisk to keep smooth. Bring to a boil, stirring constantly until sauce begins to thicken. Boil for 2 minutes, continuing to stir. Remove from heat and cool.

Alternatives & Substitutions

Serve with melted butter, curry cream sauce (recipe above) or brown gravy.

Yield 2-3 servings

Bakaður Fiskur

This baked fish is an easy and flavorful casserole-style entrée with onions and cheese

Ingredients

1 pound cod, haddock, flounder or sole fillet

1/2 teaspoon salt

1 medium onion, diced

1 tablespoon bread crumbs

2 tablespoons grated cheese

2 tablespoons butter

Instructions

1. Preheat oven to 350°
2. Cut fish into 2" chunks and place in a greased casserole dish.
3. Sprinkle with salt and diced onion.
4. Cover with bread crumbs and grated cheese.
5. Dot with small pieces of butter.
6. Bake for 20-30 minutes.

Alternatives & Substitutions

Any type cheese such as Cheddar, Swiss, or American, or a blend of several cheeses can be used.

Works well with any type of fish.

Yield 2-3 servings

Flatkökur

Flatbread is the oldest type of bread made in Iceland – dating back to 874 AD. It was originally baked on an overturned pot directly over the fire embers

Ingredients

1 1/4 cups rye flour

1 2/3 cups all-purpose flour

1/4 teaspoon baking powder

1/8 teaspoon salt

1 2/3 cups very hot water

Instructions

1. In a large bowl, sift together flour, baking powder and salt.

2. Add the hot water and mix with a spoon until dough is stiff.

3. Turn out onto a lightly floured surface and knead until dough is smooth and does not crack as you work with it. It should not stick to the surface.

4. Separate into five balls.

5. Roll out or flatten with your hand and form to make round cakes approximately 8" in diameter.

6. Perforate each side liberally with a fork to prevent air bubbles.

7. Cook over medium heat using an 8" or 9" cast-iron skillet or metal pan. Do not use butter or oil. The cooking process is closer to baking than frying.

8. Cook for 3-4 minutes, or until black spots appear on the side facing down, then turn and bake for an additional 2-3 minutes.

9. Remove from pan, dip quickly into lukewarm water and stack, covering with a damp cloth to prevent drying.

Alternatives & Substitutions

It is recommended to use flatbread within 2-3 day of making, store in refrigerator or freeze. If kept at room temperature, it will ferment within a few days.

Yield approximately 5 flatbreads

Rúgbrauð Svart

This traditional bread is sweet, heavy and hearty, excellent with a main dish or to make a sandwich

Ingredients

1 cup all-purpose white flour

1 cup whole wheat flour

1 cup rye flour

1 1/2 teaspoon baking powder

1 teaspoon baking soda

1/2 teaspoon salt

3/4 cup dark corn syrup

1 cup sour cream

1 cup buttermilk

Instructions

1. Heat oven to 250°. Grease a 5x9 bread loaf pan.
2. In a large bowl, blend together buttermilk, sour cream, and corn syrup.
3. In a separate bowl, mix flours, baking powder, baking soda and salt.
4. Add the dry ingredients to buttermilk mixture and blend completely.
5. Pour into prepared loaf pan.
6. Bake for 3 hours.
7. Remove from oven, cool completely on wire rack.

Alternatives & Substitutions

This bread freezes very well.

Yield 1 loaf

Rúgbrauð Brúnt

This hearty alternative to traditional black bread has heavier grain and is very dense. It is best stored and served at room temperature

Ingredients

2 cups all-purpose flour

1 1/4 cup whole wheat flour

1/2 tablespoon salt

1 1/2 tablespoons baking powder

3/4 milk

1/3 honey

1 cup shredded carrots (about 3 medium carrots)

1 1/4 cups rye flour

1/2 cup oatmeal

1/2 cup flax

1 1/2 tablespoons baking soda

1 1/4 cups buttermilk

Instructions

1. Preheat oven to 350°. Thoroughly grease two 9" x 5" bread pans using shortening, cooking oil or butter. Evenly coat bottom and sides of pans.

2. In a large bowl, mix the flours, oatmeal, salt, flax, baking powder and baking soda.

3. Add the milk and buttermilk and mix well. Add honey and blend. Using a manual grater or food processer, shred carrots to make one cup. Add to the batter and mix completely. Batter will be very stiff at this point. You can mix with a spoon or knead to blend.

4. Evenly divide the batter between the two prepared pans. Bake for 40-50 minutes.

5. Allow the bread to cool slightly in pan before turning out on a wire rack to cool completely.

6. This bread is best enjoyed at room temperature.

Alternatives & Substitutions

Plain yogurt can be substituted for buttermilk

This bread freezes very well.

Yield 2 loaves

Litlabollur

Icelandic Donut Balls are much larger than the American donut holes with a light sweet flavor

Ingredients

4 cups flour

1 cup sugar

4 teaspoons baking powder

2 eggs

1 1/2 cups milk

1/2 cup raisins

Instructions

1. Preheat deep fryer to the highest setting.

2. In a large bowl, blend together the flour, sugar and baking powder.

3. Add eggs and milk, mixing well using a spoon or whisk. Batter should be smooth but not thin. An electric mixer is not recommended because it may thin the batter too much.

4. Mix in raisins.

5. Using two large tablespoons, scoop and drop batter into fryer.

6. Turn as they fry until they are golden brown on all sides.

7. Drain on paper towel.

Alternatives & Substitutions

Serve plain, or sprinkle with powdered sugar or cinnamon sugar.

Can be eaten hot or cold and freeze well.

Yield approximately 48

Kleinur

This popular treat is eaten any time of day and is a staple in any Icelandic home

Ingredients

3 eggs

1 1/2 cups sugar

1 cup sour cream

1 cup whole milk or buttermilk

1 teaspoon vanilla

2 teaspoons baking soda

5 1/2 cups of flour, separated

1 teaspoon salt

1 teaspoon cream of tartar

1 teaspoon cardamom

Instructions

1. In a large bowl, mix eggs and sugar until smooth. In a separate bowl, mix the sour cream, baking soda, vanilla and buttermilk. In a third bowl, sift together 5 cups of the flour (reserve ½ cup), with the salt, cardamom, and cream of tartar.

2. Alternating between the buttermilk mixture and the flour mixture, gradually add both to the egg mixture. Stir to blend completely.

3. On a flat surface, sprinkle with the remaining ½ cup of flour. Turn out onto flour and knead for one minute. Dough will be slightly sticky.

4. Divide into three portions. Roll each out to about ¼" thick and cut into strips approximately 1" wide by 2 ½" long*. Cut a slit in the center of each and fold one end through the slit.

5. Fry in deep pan or fryer at highest setting for approximately 3 minutes, or until golden brown, turning them halfway through frying.

6. Cool on paper towel to absorb excess oil.

7. Serve plain or sprinkled with powdered sugar or cinnamon sugar. Store in sealed container or freeze up to three months.

Alternatives & Substitutions

Because kleinur requires frying at a very high temperature, when using a fryer, allow the oil time to heat up again after each round of doughnuts. *If you make this recipe often, a Fattigmann Cookie Cutter tool will make the process much easier.

Yield approximately 60

Piparkökur

Icelandic pepper cookies are very light and crispy with a mild pepper flavor

Ingredients

1 1/4 cups butter, softened

1 1/4 cups sugar

3/4 cup light corn syrup

2 eggs

3 cups all-purpose flour

1 1/2 teaspoons baking powder

1 teaspoon baking soda

1/2 teaspoon salt

2 teaspoons ground cinnamon

2 teaspoons ground cloves

1 teaspoon ground ginger

1/4 teaspoon ground black pepper

Instructions

1. In a large bowl, cream butter and sugar until smooth. Beat in the corn syrup and eggs, mixing well after each addition.

2. In a separate bowl, sift together the flour, baking powder, baking soda, salt, cinnamon, cloves, ginger, and pepper. Add dry ingredients to the butter mixture, and mix until smooth.

3. The dough will be very soft. Cover with plastic wrap and refrigerate at least 3 hours or overnight.

4. Preheat oven to 350°. Line baking sheets with parchment or paper. Roll dough into ½" balls and place on prepared baking sheet at least 2" apart.

5. Place ½ cup of flour in a shallow dish, the using a smooth-bottom glass, dip into the flour and press the cookies flat.

6. Dough will be sticky, so dip the glass in flour after each press. Cookies will grow larger when in the oven, so be sure to keep them spaced even after they are pressed.

7. Bake for 10 minutes. Remove from oven and cool on baking racks. When cool, gently peel the cookies from the wax paper. They will be very thin and crisp. Store in cookie jar or sealed container.

Alternatives & Substitutions

Yield approximately 60

Parisarkökur

The name means Parisian cookie and is a modern twist on a traditional meringue cookie

Ingredients

Cookie

>1 cup butter, softened

>1/2 cup sugar

>2 egg yolks (keep the whites for the meringue)

>2 3/4 cups all-purpose flour

Meringue

>3 egg whites

>1 cup sugar

Filling

>Raspberry Jam

Instructions

1. In a large bowl, cream butter and sugar, mixing until smooth. Carefully separate the eggs, keeping the whites in a separate bowl and set aside. Add egg yolks to the butter and sugar, mixing well and then add flour. Stir until combined.

2. Turn out dough onto a floured surface. Roll to ½" thickness and cut out to approximately 2 ½" diameter using a round cookie cutter or overturned glass.

3. Place on baking sheet about 2" apart. Place ½ teaspoonful of jam into the middle of each cookie.

4. Return to the bowl with the egg whites and sugar. Whip until stiff and meringue has a shiny texture. Place the meringue into a pastry bag with large tip.

5. Use the pastry bag to pipe circles of meringue around the edge of each cookie.

6. Bake at 300° for 16-18 minutes or until meringue is set but not browned. Test the cookie for doneness by lifting slightly to ensure bottom is lightly browned.

7. Remove from oven and cool on baking racks. Store in cookie jar or sealed container.

Alternatives & Substitutions

Mom remembers this one from her summers at her Grandpa's farm, except when they made these, it was meringue with jam in the center and no cookie underneath. Try this very quick and easy alternative!

Vanilluhringir

A traditional vanilla cookie, this buttery treat is light and crisp with just a hint of sweetness.

Ingredients

1 1/4 cup sugar

1 1/2 cup butter, softened

1 egg

2 teaspoon vanilla

3 1/3 cup flour

1/2 teaspoon baking powder

1/2 teaspoon baking soda

Instructions

1. In a medium bowl, cream butter and sugar. Add egg and vanilla and blend.

2. Add flour, baking powder, and baking soda stirring until blended completely. Divide into three balls, wrap each in plastic wrap and refrigerate for at least an hour.

3. When dough is chilled, roll out onto lightly floured surface, working with one section at a time. Dough will be easier to work with before it warms.

4. Preheat oven to 325°

5. Cut rolled dough into rounds using cutter and transfer to non-stick baking tray lined with non-stick paper.

6. Cut a slit in each cookie and separate to make center hole. Use fork to create lined design or use line-embossed rolling pin for design.

7. Bake for 12-14 minutes or until brown. Remove from oven and cool on wire racks.

Alternatives & Substitutions

Many old recipes for cookies, especially a crisp cookie, may call for "salt of hartshorn" (also referred to as "ammonium carbonate" or "baker's ammonia"). For each one (1) tablespoon of hartshorn, substitute either two (2) tablespoons of baking powder or one (1) tablespoon EACH of baking powder and baking soda.

Yield approximately 72

Mömmukökur

"Mama's cookies" are a light crispy cookie sandwiched with sweet cream filling

Ingredients

- 1/2 cup butter or margarine
- 1/3 cup light corn syrup
- 1/2 cup sugar
- 1 egg
- 4 cups flour
- 2 teaspoons baking soda
- 1 teaspoon powdered ginger
- 1 portion (batch) butter icing

See next page for Smjörkrem - Butter Icing

Instructions

1. Place the sugar, butter and corn syrup in a small pan over medium heat. Blend using wire whisk until butter is melted and mixture is smooth. Let cool completely then stir in the egg.

2. In a medium bowl, sift together flour, baking soda, and ginger. Add in the syrup mixture and knead until smooth.

3. Cover with plastic wrap and refrigerate overnight.

4. Preheat oven to 400°

5. Roll out on a floured surface and cut into circles using cookie cutters or an overturned glass, making sure there is an even number of cookies.

6. Bake for 10 minutes or until brown. Remove from oven and cool on wire racks.

7. Cool completely before adding icing and assembling sandwich cookie. See Recipe for Butter Icing.

Alternatives & Substitutions

Add ½ tablespoon of cocoa to dough for chocolate cookies and pair with coffee flavored butter icing.

Yield approximately 60 sandwich cookies

Smjörkrem

This butter icing is perfect for Mömmukökur and for layering in cakes

Ingredients

1/2 cup butter or margarine, softened

1 – 1 1/2 cup powdered sugar

1 egg yolk

1 tablespoon cream

1 tablespoon vanilla or almond extract (or other flavorings)

Food coloring, optional*

> *Using cake gel coloring instead of food coloring will make icing thicker and will hold up better if using in layer cakes

Instructions

1. Mix butter and sugar until light and fluffy.
2. Add powdered sugar and mix until smooth.
3. Add the egg yolk and cream.
4. Add flavoring and food coloring, if using.
5. Mix until smooth.

Alternatives & Substitutions

You can reduce the amount of powdered sugar to 1 cup to reduce sweetness.

Cream will make the icing smooth but can be eliminated.

Substitute flavorings with 1 tablespoon cocoa for chocolate flavor

Flavorings such as hazelnut, strawberry, peppermint or rosewater can be used to compliment fruit layers in Tertas or use as frosting on cakes (see Vinaterta)

Substitute 1 tablespoon strong coffee in place of flavorings to pair with chocolate layer.

Yield 1 portion

Bolludagur Bollur

These are traditionally made for Bun Day—the Monday before Ash Wednesday, but so easy to make anytime

Ingredients

1 cup water

1/2 cup butter

1/2 teaspoon salt

1/4 cup sugar

1 cup flour

3 large eggs

1 cup heavy whipping cream

2 tablespoons vanilla extract

2 Tablespoon powdered sugar

1/4 cup raspberry jam

7 ounces chocolate (optional)

Instructions

1. Preheat oven to 375°F. Prepare baking sheet by lining with parchment paper or greasing lightly.

2. In a large saucepan over medium heat, add the water, butter, salt and sugar, stirring until the butter is melted. Add flour and beat quickly until mixture thickens and pulls away from the side of the pan. Remove pan from heat.

3. Whisk in eggs, one at a time, beating until batter is the consistency of thick pudding.

4. Drop by heaping tablespoons onto prepared baking sheet.

5. Bake for 30 minutes or until golden brown. Do not open oven door until baking time is finished. Cool on wire rack.

6. When buns are cool, mix heavy whipping cream with vanilla extract and powdered sugar.

7. Slice each bun in half. Spread lower half with raspberry jam and top with whipped cream. Replace top of bun and dust with powdered sugar. Drizzle with chocolate. If desired.

Alternatives & Substitutions

Substitute premade whipped topping or non-dairy topping if desired.

Yield approximately 36

Rjómaterta

Literally "Whipped Cream Cake" this almond-flavored layer cake is rich with fruit and cream. A delicious traditional treat.

Ingredients

Cake

- 1 cup butter
- 4 eggs (**separated**)
- 1 cup ground almonds
- 1/2 teaspoon baking powder
- 1 cup sugar
- 1 teaspoon vanilla
- 1 cup flour

Filling

- 1/2 cup strawberry jam

Frosting (Whipped Cream)

- 1 cup heavy whipping cream
- 2 tablespoons vanilla extract
- 2 tablespoons powdered sugar

Instructions

1. Preheat oven to 350°. Grease and flour three 8" cake pans, set aside.

2. Cream butter and sugar. Separate the eggs, putting aside the whites in a separate bowl. Beat in **only** the yolks, one at a time, mixing well after each addition. Stir in vanilla and almonds.

3. Sift together the flour & baking powder and gradually add to batter.

4. From the bowl set aside, beat the egg whites until stiff. Gently fold into the batter.

5. Pour into prepared pans. Batter will make very thin layers. Bake for 30 minutes or till golden brown.

6. Cool at least 5 minutes before removing from pans.

7. Mix heavy whipping cream with vanilla extract and powdered sugar.

8. To assemble the terta, place the first cake layer on a plate or cake stand. Spread with half the strawberry jam on the cake and top with 1/3 of the frosting. Place second cake layer on top. Spread with remaining jam and the second 1/3 of frosting. Add the final layer and cover with remaining frosting.

Alternatives & Substitutions

Any type of jam or preserves can be used. Use different flavorings in the cream layer to create unique tertas or use Smjörkrem recipe in place of the frosting here. In this recipe, do not substitute non-dairy whipped topping.

Vínarterta

A traditional 7-layer treat that is surprisingly easy and not too sweet. The perfect Icelandic treat to pair with coffee.

Ingredients

Filling
- 24 ounces pitted prunes*
- 1 teaspoon ground cardamom
- 1/2 cup sugar
- 1 tablespoon lemon juice
- 1 teaspoon vanilla extract
- 1/2 teaspoon cinnamon

Cookie Layer
- 1 cup butter, softened
- 2 eggs
- 1/2 teaspoon ground cardamom
- 1 teaspoon vanilla extract
- 1/2 cup milk
- 1 1/2 cup sugar
- 4 cups flour
- 1 teaspoon baking powder
- 1 tablespoon almond extract

Icing Glaze
- 1/2 cup powdered sugar
- 2 tablespoon water (adjust as needed)

Instructions

1. Using a food processor, blend prunes to a thick paste. Place in a medium bowl. Add lemon juice, cardamom, vanilla, sugar and cinnamon and mix well. Refrigerate until ready to assemble Vínarterta

2. In one large bowl, cream the butter and sugar together. Beat in eggs one at a time. In a smaller bowl, mix together the milk, vanilla extract and almond extract. In third bowl, mix together the flour, cardamom and baking powder.

3. Add a third of your dry ingredients to the creamed butter bowl and mix well. Then, add a third of the milk mixture to the butter bowl and mix well. Continue to alternate adding dry ingredients and wet ingredients to the butter bowl until everything is mixed together and batter is smooth.

4. Divide dough into 7 small balls, cover in plastic wrap and refrigerate for 1 hour.

5. Preheat oven to 350°. To prepare baking surface for seven layers, measure and cut parchment or baking sheets into seven 8"x 8" squares.

6. Place one baking square on flat surface and lightly dust with flour. Place one dough ball in center and gently roll thin until dough covers entire surface just to edge. Repeat with second sheet and second dough ball, continuing until all seven are complete.

7. Bake each layer for 10-12 minutes until firm, but not brown. Layers can be baked two at a time by placing them side by side on a single baking sheet. Transfer baking sheets to wire rack to cool completely.

8. To assemble, warm prune filling to room temperature. Start with a cookie layer, cover completely with a generous, but not thick, layer of filling. Top with another cookie layer and cover with filling. Continue until all seven layers are stacked. The top layer can be covered with a thin icing glaze.

Alternatives & Substitutions

*If using dried prunes, cook them with 1-2 cups of water in large saucepan over medium heat until soft. Then, blend them in a food processor to make a paste.

Icing glaze: 1 cup powdered sugar and 1-2 tablespoons of water. Mix until combined and smooth.

Cake should be covered in plastic wrap and stored in a cool, dry place for at least 3 day prior to serving. Store up to 4 weeks.

Yield approximately 36

Process Steps Photos

Measure parchment or baking paper to an 8" x 8" square. Tape to the work area. Very lightly flour or use a small dusting of powdered sugar, just enough to keep the dough from sticking to the paper or rolling pin.

Using a light touch, gently roll the dough to the edges of the baking paper.

Dough will be soft and you can use the back of your hand to adjust the edges. Making the edges in line with the paper will ensure that when you assemble the terta, there will be little cutting to make the edges match.

Remove tape from the paper and place the baking sheet directly on the cookie sheet or baking tray. You can bake two at a time, placing them side by side on a baking sheet.

When all the layers are baked and cooled, assemble with one cookie layer stacked on top of one another.

The filling layer will be between each cookie layer.

Use a light icing glaze on the top, if desired. Cool completely and cut into squares.

Fyltur Hveitibrauðskrans

A beautiful coffee wreath great for breakfast or with coffee.

Ingredients

Dough:

- 2 tablespoons active dry yeast
- 1/2 cup warm water
- 1 egg
- 1/4 cup butter
- 1/3 cup sugar
- 1/4 teaspoon salt
- 1/3 cup sour cream
- 2-1/2 to 3 cups flour

Filling

- 1 cup almond paste
- 1 egg
- 2 tablespoons sugar
- 1 tablespoon cinnamon
- 1 teaspoon vanilla
- 1/2 cup raisins
- 1 tablespoon grated orange peel

Glaze

- 1 egg, slightly beaten
- 2 tablespoons milk
- Pearl sugar or crushed sugar cubes

Instructions

1. In a large bowl, dissolve the yeast in the water and let stand five minutes. Add the egg, butter, sugar, salt, and sour cream and mix well. Beat in two cups of the flour to make a stiff dough. Cover and let rise in a warm place until doubled, about 1 hour.

2. While dough is rising, prepare the filling. Blend the almond paste, egg, sugar, cinnamon, and vanilla.

3. Preheat oven to 400°. Lightly grease a baking sheet or cover with parchment paper or baking paper.

4. Once the dough has risen, turn out onto lightly floured board and roll out to make a square about 16-18" across. Spread the filling on dough to within 1/2" of the edge of the dough. Sprinkle with the raisins and orange peel. Roll dough up tightly, jelly roll fashion, enclosing the filling.

5. Carefully place the coffee roll on the pan and shape into a circle, sealing the ends together. With a pair of scissors, cut 2" slits every inch or so, lifting the cut dough back so the filling is visible. Let rise 1 hour or until nearly doubled in size.

6. To make the glaze, mix the beaten egg well with the two tablespoons milk.

7. Brush wreath with the mixture and sprinkle with the pearl sugar. Bake for 20 to 30 minutes or until golden brown.

Alternatives & Substitutions

Instead of using a pearl sugar glaze, a drizzle of icing can be used. Follow instructions for Vínarterta glaze. Eliminate the beaten egg, milk and sugar from this recipe.

Vínarbrauð I

This traditional breakfast is a favorite and the basic recipe can be made with a variety of flavors and fillings.

Ingredients

Pastry

    1 1/2 cups sugar

    1 cup milk

    8 cups flour

    1 1/2 cups butter, softened

    4 teaspoons baking powder

Filling

    8 ounces cream cheese, softened

    2 egg yolks, at room temperature

    1 teaspoon vanilla extract

    1/3 cup sugar

    2 tablespoons ricotta cheese

    Rhubarb jam (can be substituted)

Icing

    4 cups powdered sugar

    1 teaspoon vanilla or almond flavoring

    4-5 tablespoons water

    3-4 drops red food color

Instructions

1. Preheat oven to 350°. In a large bowl, cream butter and sugar. Add milk and stir. Add baking powder and flour and mix by hand. Batter will be very soft and may be sticky.

2. Generously flour a flat surface and turn out dough. Gently knead and work in just enough flour so that the dough is not too sticky, but not too much or the pastry will be tough and tasteless.

3. Divide into 3 portions. Prepare three sections of parchment or baking paper to the width of the baking sheet. Work with one sheet at a time.

4. On a clean flat work surface, tape down the edges of the paper. Lightly dust with powdered sugar to prevent sticking. Place one portion of the dough in the center of the paper. Lightly roll out the dough to a rectangle approximately 6-7" wide and 11-12" long. Dough will be very pliable so you can use the back edge of your hand to form the shape.

5. For the filling, combine cream cheese, sugar, egg yolks, ricotta cheese and vanilla and blend. On the prepared pastry, spread a generous amount of the cream cheese filling down center from top to bottom, stopping about 1" from each edge. Add a line of jam on top of the cream cheese filling. Fold over each side towards the middle, but leave about 1/2" gap in the center.

6. Move entire baking paper onto cooking sheet and bake for 12-15 minutes or until edges are lightly brown. Cool on wire racks. Prepare icing while baking. Allow pastry to cool slightly, then apply a line of icing down the center.

Alternatives & Substitutions

Yield 3 pastries, approximately 6-8 slices each.

Vínarbrauð II

This version has a light cinnamon sugar filling and a smooth sweet icing

Ingredients

Pastry

- 1 cup butter
- 2 eggs
- 2 cups flour
- 1 cup sugar
- 2 teaspoons baking powder
- 2/3 cup cinnamon sugar, divided

Icing

- 1 cup powdered sugar
- 1 teaspoon vanilla extract
- 2 1/4 teaspoon water
- 1 teaspoon butter, melted
- 1/2 teaspoon corn syrup
- 2-3 drops red food coloring or 1/2 tablespoon cocoa for chocolate frosting

Instructions

1. Preheat oven to 350°. In a large bowl, cream butter and sugar. Add eggs and stir. Add baking powder and flour and mix by hand. Batter will be very soft and may be sticky.

2. Flour a flat surface and turn out dough. Gently knead and work in just enough flour so that the dough can be rolled. Divide into 3 portions. Prepare three sections of parchment or baking paper to the width of the baking sheet. Work with one sheet at a time.

3. On a clean flat work surface, tape down the edges of the baking paper. Lightly dust with powdered sugar to prevent sticking. Place one portion of dough in the center of the paper. Lightly roll out the dough to a rectangle approximately 6-7" wide and 11-12" long. Dough will be very pliable so you can use the back edge of your hand to form the shape.

4. Sprinkle 2 Tablespoons of the cinnamon sugar down the center, completely top to bottom, but stopping about 1" from the side edges. Fold over each side towards the middle, but leave about 1/2" gap in the center.

5. Move entire baking paper onto cooking sheet and bake for 15-17 minutes or until edges are lightly brown. Cool on wire racks.

6. Prepare icing while baking. Allow pastry to cool slightly, then apply a line of icing down the center. Cool completely before serving.

Alternatives & Substitutions

Yield 3 pastries, approximately 6-8 slices each.

Vínarbrauð III

This is a large recipe, perfect for making several pastries with a variety of fillings and icings.

Ingredients

1 cup butter or margarine

2 cups sugar

2 egg

1 cup milk

1/2 tablespoon lemon juice

1 tablespoon vanilla

3 teaspoons baking powder

1/2 teaspoon salt

6 cups flour

1 jar rhubarb jam, or other flavor of jam or preserves

Chocolate for drizzling if desired

Instructions

1. In a large bowl, cream butter and sugar. Add eggs, milk, lemon juice and vanilla and mix well.

2. Add the flour, baking powder and salt and mix with spoon until dough is stiff. Turn out on lightly floured board and knead until smooth.

3. Separate dough into three equal parts. Set two parts aside.

4. Cut sheets of parchment or baking paper to fit baking sheet

5. Taking the first part, roll and flatten into a square approximately 9". Cut the square into three equal-width strips. Carefully transfer each strip to baking paper. Once transferred, place a line of jam along the center 1/3 of the dough from top to bottom stopping about 1" from the edge. Fold ends towards the center but leave about 1/2" gap so the ends do not touch. Move parchment paper to baking sheet.

6. Repeat with remaining two strips. You may put more than one sheet on a tray, but no not overlap. Repeat entire process with remaining two sections of dough. Total yield will be nine Vínarbrauð

7. Bake at 350° for about 15 minutes or until the strips just begin to brown. Cool slightly and immediately put a thick strip of icing down the center only. Cool completely. Store in sealed container.

Alternatives & Substitutions

Each pastry can be made with different fillings of jam, almond paste, cream cheese filling or a combination. Yield 9 pastries, approximately 6-8 slices each. Freezes well.

Púðingur Fylta

Custard is a common topping used on Vínarbrauð along with icing

Ingredients

2 cups milk

1/4 cup cornstarch

1/4 cup sugar + 2 tablespoons sugar

2 egg yolks* + 1 egg

2 tablespoons butter

1 teaspoon vanilla

Instructions

1. In a medium bowl, whisk the egg and two egg yolks. In a separate bowl, mix the 2 tablespoons sugar with the cornstarch. Gradually add to the eggs and whisk until smooth then set aside.

2. In a medium saucepan, slowly heat the milk with 1/4 cup sugar until at a boil, stirring to keep from burning

3. Very slowly, gradually pour the heated milk into the eggs, while whisking constantly. The mixture should be warm but not hot enough to cook the eggs. Whisk vigorously to maintain smooth texture.

4. Pour mixture back into saucepan and return to a medium heat.

5. Stir constantly as mixture cooks to keep it from sticking or burning. It will begin to thicken just as it starts to boil. Allow the boil to start then remove from heat

6. Mix in butter and vanilla, whisking until completely smooth and blended. Pour into glass or metal bowl. Cover with plastic directly against the surface of the custard to prevent a skin from forming.

7. Refrigerate until completely chilled and firm before using on Vínarbrauð.

Alternatives & Substitutions

* Use the egg whites for a wash over pastry, top with coarse sugar for an alternative topping. This will also give the pastry a more browned finish.

Pönnukökur

A very thin pancake typically filled with jam and whipped cream or even cinnamon sugar. Served folded in quarters or rolled.

Ingredients

4 tablespoons butter or margarine, softened

1/3 cup sugar

2 eggs

2 teaspoons vanilla

2 1/2 cups flour

1 teaspoon baking powder

1/2 teaspoon salt

1/4 teaspoon baking soda

2 1/4 cups milk

Instructions

1. In a large bowl, cream the butter or margarine and sugar. Add eggs and vanilla, blending well.

2. Add in the flour, baking powder, salt and baking soda and mix thoroughly.

3. Gradually add in milk, frequently scraping edge of bowl to maintain a smooth consistency. Batter will be very thin.

4. Heat an 8" flat-bottom frying pan or cast iron skillet. Test for readiness by dripping drops of water – pan is ready when water sizzles as soon as it hits the pan.

5. Remove pan from heat to pour 1/4 cup of batter, tipping pan to spread completely across bottom. Batter should lightly cover the surface of the pan.

6. Return to stovetop burner and cook for 20-30 seconds until browned. Turn and cook 20-30 seconds on the opposite side.

7. Stack and serve.

Alternatives & Substitutions

Pönnukökur is typically served at room temperature, with a section of jams, whipped cream and cinnamon sugar.

Freezes well

Yield about 15

Visit our website for all books by our authors:

www.heklapublishing.com

Other Books by Ieda Herman
Follow me: www.vikingamma.com

Growing Up Viking: Fond Memories of Iceland
Viking Kids Don't Cry
Ambassadors of Orealis Trilogy Book 1: The Silver Arrow
Ambassadors of Orealis Trilogy Book 2: Inner Space Aliens (November 2017)

Other Books by Heidi Herman
www.heidihermanauthor.com

The Guardians of Iceland and Other Icelandic Folk Tales
Legend of the Icelandic Yule Lads
Icelandic Yule Lads Mayhem at the North Pole
Icelandic Yule Lads & Other Legends Activity Book
Her Viking Heart (December, 2017)

ABOUT THE AUTHORS

At 91, she's still on the run! Íeda graduated from the Chicago School of Interior Design and later the Institute of Children's Literature, in Connecticut. She has written numerous articles for newspaper and magazines, and has conducted community college adult education seminars. Her natural enthusiasm has energized seminars participants at libraries, schools, women's clubs, and community groups. After retiring in 2009, and with her family grown, Íeda wrote her memoirs, and has since continued to write and share stories about Iceland. Her second book, a young adult fiction adventure based in Iceland was released in 2016.

Born and raised in Iceland, Íeda instilled her love of life and adventure in each of her ten children. The youngest, Heidi, has joined her on adventures in Iceland. There, they have gone paragliding, hiking through the cave that inspired Jules Verne's *Journey to the Center of the Earth,* ridden Icelandic horses through the mountains and explored famous sites from the Sagas like Snorri Sturlson's home (and site of his murder!) Back in the States, together they host presentations about Iceland to clubs, community groups and speak at special events.

Heidi is a native of Illinois with a proud Scandinavian heritage. Having an Icelandic mother, she grew up with stories of brave fishermen, mischievous trolls and adventurous Vikings. After a career in telecom consulting, Heidi was inspired by her mother's memoirs, moving from training classes and technical writing to once again being immersed in the childhood fascination of legend, lore and imaginative stories. She turned her focus to fiction writing, researching and modernizing Icelandic folk tales and stories from the Sagas. She has published four children's books based on Icelandic folklore.

www.ingramcontent.com/pod-product-compliance
Lightning Source LLC
Chambersburg PA
CBHW051354110526
44592CB00024B/2984